Here are

101

tips for you to grow up happy and successful.

To get the best out of life,

AIM HIGH!

www.aimhigh101tipsforteens.com

Inquiries Contact:
bradberger29@gmail.com

Book designed by Larry Rubenstein

ISBN: 978-1-60702-242-8

This book is for you.
It is for teenagers
everywhere.

The 101 Tips in this book
will make you a happier
person and a better person.

You already know many
of the tips and they are
part of your life.

AIM HIGH! is your guide
for school and life.

TABLE OF CONTENTS

Think!

Think before
you do something.

Consider the
alternatives before
you act.

Careful thinking
produces the best
results.

**Ethics and morals
are important.**

Ethics are the moral
standards and rules
of correct conduct.

An ethical person
has the ability to pick
and choose the
proper way to act.

Take pride in
acting correctly.

Have a positive attitude.

Be a positive person.

You can think only one thought at a time – make it a positive one.

Look for the positive in every experience, situation, and person.

3

Develop your goals.

Goals are what you want to achieve.

Make a plan, and imagine yourself achieving your goals.

Your imagination and your work each day will help you achieve your goals.

4

Persistence pays.

Persistent people accomplish what they set out to do.

They act consistently until they reach a goal.

Persistent people achieve their goals.

5

Make commitments, keep your word.

Follow through on the commitments you make.

Keeping commitments earns respect and trust from others.

You will become a stronger and better person if you keep your word.

6

Tell the truth.

Telling the truth is the right way to act.

Living with lies is harder than living a truthful life.

Being truthful and honest is important.

Make a good impression.

Always make a good impression.

Put your best foot forward.

First impressions are very important.

Neatness counts.

It is easier to function in a neat and orderly space instead of a mess.

You will feel better when your appearance and your environment are neat.

9

Be healthy.

Develop habits that keep you healthy.

Maintaining good health is your decision and a lifelong choice.

You can make yourself healthy.

10

Keep your hands clean; wash them as often as possible.

Clean hands help to keep you healthy.

Wash your hands with soap and water for at least 15 seconds.

Keep your hands clean. Keep yourself healthy.

11

**Eat fruits and
vegetables, they are
good for you.**

Eat fruits and vegetables
each and every day.

They will energize you,
control your weight,
and keep you healthy.

Seven is the lucky
number of fruits and
veggies to eat each day.

Eat a good breakfast.

Start your day in
a healthy way.

Eat nutritious foods
that give you the energy
your body needs to
maintain your maximum
efficiency throughout
the day.

Breakfast keeps
you awake.

13

Don't smoke!

Never smoke.

Smoking causes cancer. It also causes heart and lung disease and other fatal diseases.

If you have started smoking, quit now.

If you can't quit, get help. You can do it!

Smoking can kill you.

Avoid drugs!

By using drugs you hurt your mind and your body, and you are breaking the law.

Maintain your health and happiness by saying "no" to drugs.

If you have a drug habit, seek help from family, friends and professionals.

15

Drive sober.

To drink, or to do drugs and to drive is a way to death.

Take a taxi, public transportation, or stay where you are.

Your parent, an adult or a friend will be much happier to pick you up anywhere when you are intoxicated rather than seeing you injured.

16

Exercise.

Exercise is important for your physical and mental well-being.

Develop an exercise routine and you acquire a healthy habit for life.

Enjoy your exercise.

17

Relax.

Take a break.

Sit by yourself in a calm and quiet place.

Close your eyes. Breathe deeply for a few minutes.

Read a book, watch a television program or listen to music.

Find a method of relaxation that works for you.

Get enough sleep.

Teenagers need more sleep than adults.

Doctors recommend that teens get between 10 and 12 hours of sleep each night.

Teenagers physically need extra sleep.

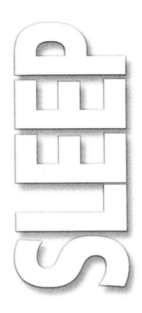

Look for the good in people and events.

Search for the good
in everyone.

You will often find more
than you expect.

Look at the sunny
side of life.

20

Respect everyone.

Respect everyone in the same way that you want to be respected.

Respecting others is the best way to earn respect for yourself.

21

**Be supportive of
your family.**

Spend time with
your family and learn
from them.

Get to know and enjoy
your relatives.

Listen to your parent or the person responsible for your care.

Think about what a parent or caring adult says to you.

If you disagree, disagree in a respectful manner.

A caring adult usually has your best interest in mind when making a decision affecting your life.

Talk to a relative.

If you have a problem, try talking to a person who loves you and wants the best for you.

A relative is often the best friend you have.

If you are going to be out late, call to let someone know.

Do not go out or stay out late without letting someone know where you are.

It is wise to be cautious.

People must be informed of where you are to protect your safety.

25

If your parents fight or separate, remember you are not at fault.

If parents fight, separate, or divorce, it's not your fault.

If you are upset, speak to a friend or a relative and consider seeking help from your school's guidance counselor or psychologist.

26

Be loyal.

Keep your loyalty to
the people you like.

Stand by their side
when they need you.

Your loyalty will
be appreciated.

27

Be a good friend.

To have a good
friend you need to
be a good friend.

Do things for and
with your friend
that you might not
do with anybody else.

Good friends are special
people.

28

**Respect the
opposite sex.**

There are many
differences and
similarities between
girls and boys,
men and women.

Respect the similarities
and differences.

29

Accept responsibility.

Take responsibility
for what you do.

Be a good person.

30

Learn in school.

Pay attention in class, respect your teachers, and learn.

Learn as much as you can.

Do your homework.

Take your time and concentrate on your homework.

If you need help, ask your friends and family.

Complete your homework on time and do your best work.

Reading is necessary.

Read something
you truly enjoy.

It could be the sports
section of a newspaper,
a magazine, or a book.

The more you read,
the easier it is to read.

Develop a good vocabulary.

To effectively convey what you feel and think, you need to learn as many words as possible.

As you learn more words, you will be able to express yourself better when either speaking or writing.

When you find a word you don't know, look it up in a dictionary; write down the definition and use the word.

Learn another language.

Learn a foreign language.

If you are lucky to live with others who speak another language, you might want to learn their language.

Learning another language will help you throughout your life.

35

Use a computer.

A computer will give you the power to do everything from playing games to communicating with people throughout the world.

Use a computer to enrich your life.

Go to movies and watch television.

It's fun to go to movies and watch television.

Be selective. See movies and programs that relax you, entertain you, and educate you.

Listen to music.

The sound of music is one of life's pleasures.

Whether it is rap, disco, hip-hop, jazz, or opera, music is beautiful.

Listen and make your own choices.

38

Get a hobby.

Your hobby is a special interest you really enjoy.

You can listen to music, collect things, paint, write, or participate in sports.

Have fun with your hobby.

39

Be creative and enjoy your creativity.

Artists, athletes, corporate presidents, and children are creative.

You can be creative in school, at home, or with your friends.

You can be creative in sports, in art, in music, with words, or with a computer.

Allow yourself to be creative.

40

Perfection.

People are not perfect.

Be happy being
yourself.

Be a nice person.

A nice person is pleasant to others.

People who are nice have a good attitude.

Being nice is nice.

Be kind.

Think about your
actions and the type of
person you want to be.

Be an understanding
and charitable person.

Kindness makes
everyone feel better.

Be fair.

What seems fair to one person may not seem fair to another.

When you are fair with people, it is more likely that they will treat you fairly.

Show appreciation.

Everyone wants to be appreciated.

Express appreciation to others.

Courtesy counts.

Hold the door for somebody. Don't push when you are standing in line. Give up your seat to an elderly person on a bus or train.

When you are courteous, people will be courteous to you.

"Please" and "thank you" are really magic words.

By saying "please" and "thank you," people show themselves to be thoughtful, respectful, and nice.

47

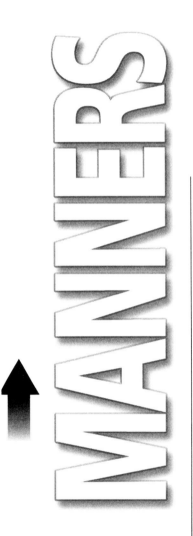

Use the best table manners.

People judge you by your manners.

Learn proper table manners.

Practice your manners, and they will become good habits.

48

Avoid rude words.

Avoid rude or crude
words that might
hurt or embarrass
other people.

Always consider
what affect your
words will have.

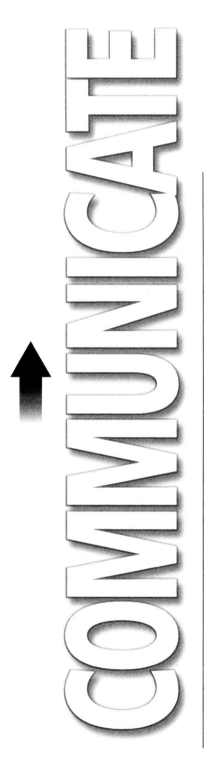

**Communicate
constructively.**

Get to the point.

Whether speaking or writing, keep your communications clear.

Speak clearly and maintain eye contact.

Don't mumble.

Look directly at the other person, maintain eye contact, and speak clearly.

When you have something to say, say it.

Speak up and then listen.

It is important to express your opinions.

There are situations that require listening.

Once you have made your point, stop talking and listen.

Ask questions.

Asking questions does not show a lack of knowledge, but rather the search for knowledge.

Ask questions in a thoughtful and polite manner.

Learn from the answers.

Listen to advice.

When a person gives you advice, listen.

You may accept or reject the advice.

The decision is yours.

54

Help others.

If you know someone
needs help, help.

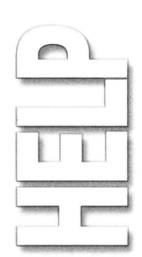

Join a team.

Join a team such as a
sports team, a club, or a
volunteer organization.

Teams teach individuals
to work and play with
others.

**Plan to win and you
will be a winner.**

Tell yourself several
times each day that you
are a winner and you
will accomplish what
you want.

A winning attitude
creates a winner.

Winning isn't always everything.

No person or team wins all the time.

Don't dwell on losses.

Look forward to the next time you will win.

Keep your confidence and your next win will be sooner than you think.

Everyone makes mistakes.

We all make mistakes.

Learn to avoid making the same mistakes twice.

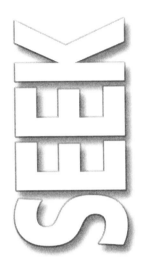

Seek help.

Don't be embarrassed
to ask for help.

People like to help
each other.

Seek help from the best
person available.

Show your appreciation
to the person helping
you.

60

Sorry.

If you hurt someone's feelings, apologize.

If you make a mistake, apologize.

Saying "I'm sorry" will make you and the other person feel better.

Learn to deal with criticism.

No one likes to be criticized.

Deal with the criticism in a positive way.

Don't blame the messenger. Just listen to the message and do your best.

Forgive.

Show forgiveness
in your heart and in
your mind.

Be a forgiving person.

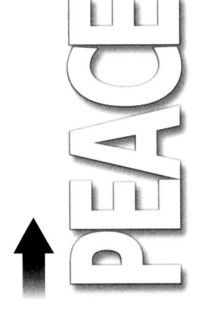

**Violence is not
the solution.**

Talk out your problems,
don't fight about them.

Listen, speak, and
resolve your differences.

Be a peaceful person.

Plan your life.

Don't leave your life to chance.

Think about what you want to achieve.

Your life belongs to you.

Follow the rules.

Know the rules
and go with them.

Breaking rules causes
punishment and other
bad stuff.

Follow rules.

Use time wisely.

Plan your activities so that you can accomplish all you want.

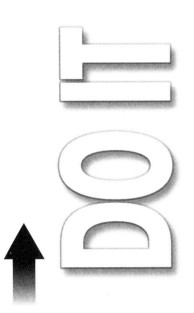

Keep motivated.

Motivation is the desire to achieve and accomplish what you want in life.

Keep yourself motivated and enjoy your progress.

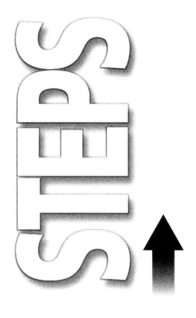

**Take one step
at a time.**

Every goal has
many steps.

Go step by step.

Accomplish something
each day and you will
accomplish what you
want in life.

**Try hard –
do your best.**

Always strive to
do your best.

Your extra efforts,
giving 100 percent,
giving it your all will
lead to the extraordinary
accomplishments in
your life.

If you try hard and
keep a positive
attitude, you will
always do your best.

Reward yourself.

When you achieve something, reward yourself.

Buy yourself a present, go to a movie, do a special fun activity.

You deserve to reward yourself when you achieve things in your life.

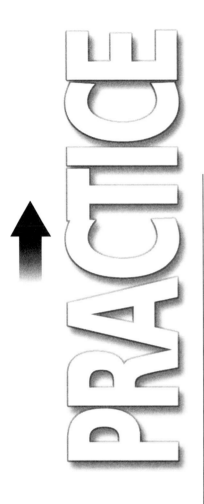

Practice, practice, practice...

To be good at anything you need to practice.

No one is a champion or a gold-medal winner without practice.

People born with extraordinary talents still must practice their skills.

Practice with a positive attitude and you will succeed.

Try, try, try again.

Work your way around obstacles.

Don't give up until you have tried all of the proper ways to achieve your goal.

Keep trying and you will succeed.

Some days are better than others.

Everyone has good and bad days.

Life is not one steady flow of good or bad events.

Try to remember the good in each day.

When things are bad, keep your positive spirit and remember tomorrow will be a better day.

Be careful.

Be careful about the way you lead your life.

Think and use good judgment in what you say and do.

Stand up for yourself.

Don't let bullies push you around.

Stand up for what you believe in, and, if you feel threatened, do not hesitate to speak to a teacher or a parent or other adult.

Be flexible.

Flexibility allows you
to adjust to change in
a constructive way.

Be flexible.

Life is full of compromises.

No one gets their way all the time.

Learn to compromise and you will get what you want most of the time.

**Don't feel sorry
for yourself.**

Bad things happen
to everyone.

Don't get stuck in
self-pity.

Focus your energies on
being positive and
regaining your spirit.

Express anger in a constructive way.

Learn to deal with anger in a constructive way and non-violent way.

Some people scream, some people rip things up, and some people keep the anger inside of them.

If you are angry at someone, let them know your feelings.

When you let go of your anger, you will feel better.

It's okay to cry.

Crying is an important expression of human emotion.

Don't be embarrassed to cry.

Presidents, athletes, and just regular people cry.

A good cry will make you feel better.

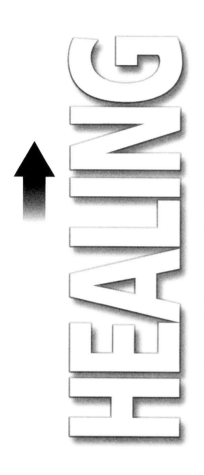

Time heals.

Some wounds take longer to heal than others.

As time passes your hurts, your injuries, and your mind and body will heal.

Have a Win/Win attitude.

Any situation is better if both people can be winners.

If you can convince another person that your position is correct and, at the same time, the other person gains something, then you have created a Win/Win situation.

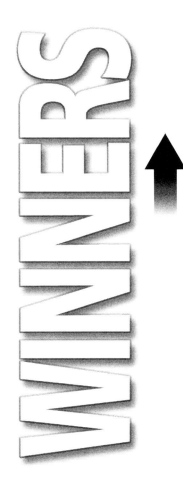

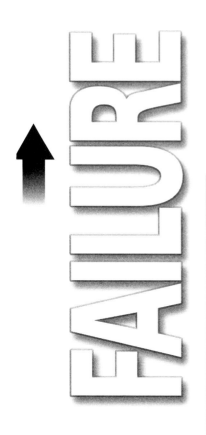

**Good people fail, but
you are not a failure.**

Failure is part of life.

Because you fail does
not make you a failure.

Learn from the failure.

Put it behind you
and move on.

Believe in yourself.

When you believe in yourself, you have the ability to do almost anything you set your mind, heart, and body to.

Have confidence in your ability to succeed, and you will.

Be enthusiastic.

Enthusiasm is the joy you show when doing your daily activities.

When you are enthusiastic, whatever you are doing becomes more pleasurable.

Enthusiasm is contagious.

86

View problems as challenges.

Problems are challenges to overcome.

Face problems and handle them quickly.

Use your creativity, imagination, common sense, and intuition to solve problems.

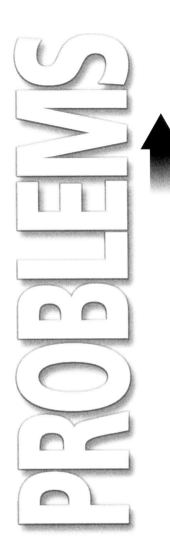

Think happy.

Think happy thoughts.

When you are down,
replace your negative
thoughts with positive,
happy thoughts.

Let your thoughts
be happy throughout
your day.

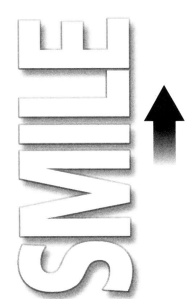

Smile.

When you smile, people around you smile with you.

A smile cheers up a room, makes a difficult situation more pleasant, and creates good feelings among people.

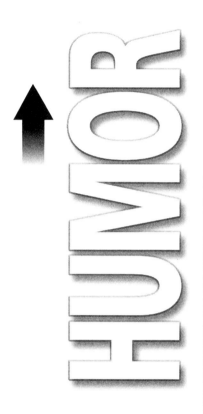

**Develop a sense
of humor.**

A sense of humor
makes both the serious
moments in life and
the lighter moments
more enjoyable.

It is good to laugh at
yourself as well as
having the ability to
enjoy another person's
humor.

Lighten up!

90

Play.

Find an activity that you enjoy and have fun doing it.

Enjoy nature.

Trees, the sky, the birds, and weather are true wonders of nature.

Take time to enjoy the natural wonders that are a part of your world.

Have heroes.

Heroes are women and men of excellence who did great things.

Model yourself after your heroes.

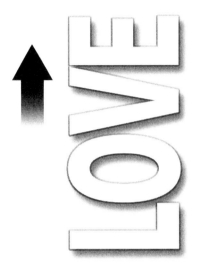

You are loved.

You are loved by many people.

People show love in different ways.

Learn to recognize different types of love.

Show love to those you love.

Dream.

Dream the possible
and the impossible.

If you dream something
often enough, it becomes
a goal in your life.

Dreams come true when
you achieve your goals.

Miracles happen.

Things happen in life that can't be explained.

Miracles do happen.

96

Begin again.

Starting something is the first step to completion.

Don't be afraid to start again.

If you don't begin, you can't reach the end.

Be proud; take pride in yourself.

Keep your positive mental attitude and try your best, and you will feel proud about yourself.

98

Be courageous.

Courage conquers fear.

Be courageous!

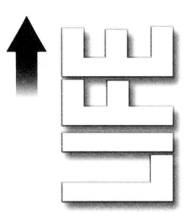

Love life.

Life is good.

Enjoy yourself
and be happy.

100

AIM HIGH!

Enjoy your life.

MY THOUGHTS...

Think!

Think!

Think!

Think!

Think!

Think!

Think!

Think!

Think!

Think!

Think!

Think!

Think!

Think!

Think!

Think!

Think!

Think!

Think!